Antarctica
THE LAST UNSPOILED CONTINENT

BY LAURENCE PRINGLE

SIMON & SCHUSTER BOOKS FOR YOUNG READERS
PUBLISHED BY SIMON & SCHUSTER
NEW YORK   LONDON   TORONTO   SYDNEY   TOKYO   SINGAPORE

"There is no place as pristinely beautiful, where the air is clearer, the grandeur more overwhelming, the animals more fascinating. If God took a vacation on this planet, He would go to the Antarctic."

FRANK S. TODD,
Polar Biologist

ACKNOWLEDGEMENTS: Thanks to editor Julie Amper, who was an enthusiastic advocate of this book since 1987; to Pam Pollack who guided it smoothly to publication; to Sylvia Frezzolini Severance for her extraordinary design; and to the scientists, photographers, and scientist-photographers—especially Stan Jacobs of the Lamont-Doherty Geophysical Laboratory—for their information and illustrations.

SIMON & SCHUSTER BOOKS FOR YOUNG READERS
Simon & Schuster Building, Rockefeller Center, 1230 Avenue of the Americas, New York, New York 10020. Copyright © 1992 by Laurence Pringle. All rights reserved including the right of reproduction in whole or in part in any form. SIMON & SCHUSTER BOOKS FOR YOUNG READERS is a trademark of Simon & Schuster. Designed by Sylvia Frezzolini. Manufactured in Hong Kong

10 9 8 7 6 5 4 3 2

LIBRARY OF CONGRESS CATALOGING-IN-PUBLICATION DATA
Pringle, Laurence P.   Antarctica: our last unspoiled continent/Laurence Pringle.
   Includes index.   Summary: Surveys the plant and animal life, impact on global ecology, history, and politics of the White Continent.   1. Antarctic regions—Juvenile literature. [1. Antarctic regions.] I. Title. G863.P75 1992 919.8'9—dc20
90-273 62   CIP   AC
ISBN 0-671-73850-x

CONTENTS

FUTURE OF A FROZEN LAND

Vast, cold, white—Antarctica is a land of contrasts. It is one of the driest places on earth, but its ice locks up more than two-thirds of our planet's freshwater. It is the quietest place on earth, but it is often blasted by roaring, hurricane-force winds. It is mostly a mass of barren ice, but its rocky and icy edges and surrounding seas nurture great numbers of penguins, seals, and other life.

Antarctica is the earth's fifth largest continent, as big as the United States and Mexico combined. But its climate is so harsh that people can only stay there by great effort and at great cost. Food and other necessities must be brought in by air or sea. Antarctica has been called "the worst place on earth."

It also has been called *terra incognita*—the unknown land. First sighted in 1820, for many decades Antarctica was ignored. Since 1956, however, Antarctica has become a unique outdoor laboratory for scientists of many nations. Some people believe it should be declared a world park with just one export: precious knowledge that scientists can find nowhere else on earth.

Antarctica is ten percent of earth's land, yet it is not owned by anyone. Now, in a world hungry for resources, many nations eye the white continent. Deposits of coal and minerals have been found; there are hints of oil.

Antarctica always challenges visitors with its frigid climate. It also challenges the world's nations to answer basic questions about its future. Should its territory be divided up? Can its resources be developed and somehow shared by all humanity? Or should Antarctica be left as it is: a wild natural laboratory?

The answer to these questions will affect everyone on earth.

Explorers saw rocks on icebergs—a clue that land lay southward beyond the barrier of sea ice. Modern ice-breaking ships can break through sea ice.

DISCOVERING THE LOST CONTINENT

Scholars in ancient Greece believed that a large mass of land existed at the bottom of the world, to balance the land at the top. In the fifteenth century, European explorers began to sail southward, looking for this continent. Over the next two centuries, ships reached the Falklands and other far southern islands.

British Captain James Cook spent three years (1772–1775) in a fruitless search for the lost continent. As he sailed around it, he saw rock debris on icebergs drifting north. This was evidence of land farther south. But Antarctica, ringed by sea ice, resisted discovery.

Again and again, Cook sailed south only to meet a barrier of ice that was impenetrable to his wooden sailing ship. His effort, however, set the stage for the discovery of Antarctica. The detailed charts of Cook's voyages, and his accounts of great numbers of fur seals, brought dozens of ships on seal hunts.

Hunters of fur seals were the first people to see Antarctica.

On island after island the sealers wiped out entire seal populations. Searching for new seal colonies, the hunters pushed farther and farther south. In 1820, crews on sealing ships from both Great Britain and the United States saw for the first time the Antarctic Peninsula, the continent's north-reaching arm.

During the 1830s, after most fur seal colonies had been wiped out, ships seeking whales began prowling the waters around Antarctica. More of the mysterious continent and its offshore islands were sighted. In the years 1838–1843, the United States, France, and Great Britain sent scientific expeditions to Antarctica.

The two ships of the British expedition, led by James Clark Ross, were specially strengthened to push through ice-covered waters. In 1841, Ross's expedition sailed close to the Antarctic coast, exploring farther south than anyone had ever been. He saw the mighty Transantarctic Mountains, and a volcano spewing flames and smoke. He named it Mount Erebus, after one of his stout ships.

Ross then made an astonishing discovery: a cliff of ice, up to 200 feet high, that seemed to stretch without end to the east. He sailed 250 miles along this huge barrier before oncoming winter brought an end to his voyage. This mass of ice is called the Ross Ice Shelf. The size of France, it is 600 miles long and between 800 and a thousand feet thick. It is the largest of many floating ice shelves that fill indentations of the Antarctic coast.

The front of the Ross Ice Shelf

Fifty-two years passed before others explored the Antarctic continent. Men of a Norwegian expedition became the first to camp overwinter on Antarctica, in 1899–1900. As the twentieth century dawned, explorers began a quest that captured worldwide public attention: reaching the South Pole.

One expedition, in 1909, had to turn back when only 97 miles from its goal. In 1911 two competing expeditions, from Norway and Great Britain, camped by the Ross Ice Shelf and prepared for a race to the South Pole, more than 800 miles inland.

On October 19 of that year, Norwegian Roald Amundsen set out with four men and 52 husky dogs that hauled sleds loaded with food, tents, and other materials. Amundsen had picked companions who were experienced skiers and dog-handlers. As they traveled they killed some dogs to feed the remaining huskies—and themselves. On December 14 they believed they had reached the South Pole, and planted the Norwegian flag.

In order to locate the Pole more precisely, Amundsen and his assistants spent three days making measurements of the sun's altitude, using a device called a sextant. At Polheim, "The Home of the Pole," as Amundsen called it, they left a tent, some supplies, and a message for those who followed. Then they headed back toward the coast. The five men and eleven surviving dogs reached their base camp on January 25, 1912, after a journey of 1,860 miles.

The British expedition, led by Robert Scott, used sled dogs and also Manchurian ponies to haul supplies. Scott's aides were not good skiers or familiar with managing sled dogs. On November 2, 1911, the poorly planned expedition set out. The ponies died on the first leg of the journey, and eventually the men themselves pulled the sleds over the vast cold polar plateau. Exhausted and running low on supplies, they reached the South Pole on January 18, 1912. There they found the flag of Norway.

"Great God," Scott wrote in his journal, "this is an awful place." Struggling back toward the coast, he and his companions learned just how awful the interior of Antarctica could be. Two men had already perished when a blizzard halted Scott and the other two on March 19, 1912. They died in their tent, just eleven miles from a cache of food and fuel.

Ice locked ships were supply bases for explorers who tried to reach the South Pole. The expedition planned and led by Robert Scott (above, standing in center) ran short of food. Exhausted from hauling sleds, all the men died while trying to return to the coast.

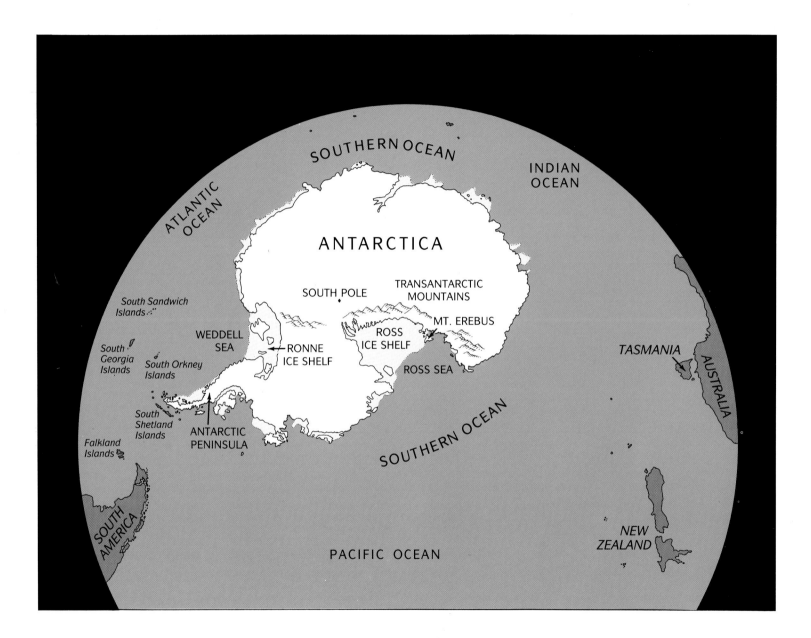

SOUTHERN OCEAN

INDIAN OCEAN

ATLANTIC OCEAN

ANTARCTICA

TRANSANTARCTIC MOUNTAINS

SOUTH POLE

MT. EREBUS

South Sandwich Islands

WEDDELL SEA

ROSS ICE SHELF

TASMANIA

AUSTRALIA

South Georgia Islands

South Orkney Islands

RONNE ICE SHELF

ROSS SEA

South Shetland Islands

ANTARCTIC PENINSULA

Falkland Islands

SOUTH AMERICA

SOUTHERN OCEAN

NEW ZEALAND

PACIFIC OCEAN

A CONTINENT FOR SCIENCE

An Argentine research station

With the race to the South Pole over, nations began to send biologists, geologists, and other scientists to explore Antarctica. The development of short wave radios, snowmobiles, and aerial photography helped scientists learn about the vast, desolate landscape. They began to investigate Antarctica's mountains, lakes, glaciers, and its fascinating life, both present and past.

Some nations began maintaining year round research stations on Antarctica, for political as well as for scientific reasons. By the mid-1950s seven countries had claimed parts of Antarctica as their territory. Five other nations, including Japan, the United States, and the former Soviet Union, also had strong interest in the continent, though they made no formal claims.

Disputes over territorial claims were put aside in 1957–1958, during an 18-month period called the International Geophysical Year, or IGY. Antarctica

was singled out for special attention by scientists during IGY. The twelve nations that were most interested in the continent launched a major effort to learn more about Antarctica. In all, scientists from 67 nations conducted research on Antarctica during IGY.

The success of this cooperative effort inspired the drafting of the Antarctic Treaty. Signed by twelve nations in 1959, it came into force in 1961 and remained in effect for 30 years.

The Antarctic Treaty declared the continent a research preserve. Nations could freely exchange scientific findings, and inspect one another's research bases whenever they wanted. Also, Antarctica was to be used only for peaceful purposes. The treaty banned military activities, the testing of weapons, and disposal of radioactive waste on the continent.

The treaty had flaws, but it set aside for at least three decades the thorny issue of territorial claims. Scientific research flourished. Antarctica still holds many mysteries, but scientists now know that it has unique value as a place to answer many questions about the earth.

Studying Antarctic wildlife, scientists lower hydrophones into water (right) to record the sounds of killer whales (left). They also catch, examine, and release Adelie penguins.

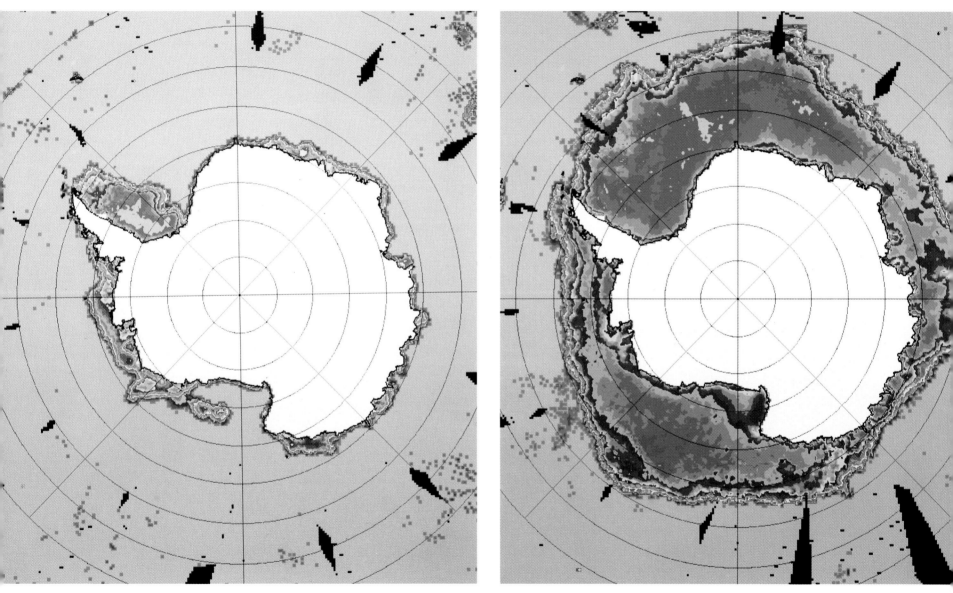

Satellite images show sea ice surrounding Antarctica at left in summer (mid-February) and at right in winter (late August). False colors show the continent as all white, open ocean as light blue, and different concentrations of ice as purple, green, and other colors.

THE WORLD'S ICEBOX

The name Antarctic means "opposite the Arctic." The two polar regions differ in more than name and place. Geographer Isaiah Bowman once said that the Arctic is a hollow and the Antarctic is a hump. In other words, the Arctic is an ocean surrounded by continents, and the Antarctic is a continent surrounded by an ocean.

This difference has a huge effect on climate. Ice on the Arctic Ocean melts each summer and the dark waters absorb heat from the sun. Year round these waters are usually warmer than the surrounding land.

In contrast, nearly all of Antarctica is ice-covered year round. It is the world's highest continent, and its high altitude contributes to its cold temperatures. Most important is the permanent mass of ice that covers most of Antarctica. The white continent reflects up to 90 percent of the sunlight it receives, so little heat is absorbed.

Although the surrounding ocean is warmer than the land, it too is covered with ice much of the year. This sea ice can be more than six feet thick. Near the end of winter (September in Antarctica), it reaches hundreds of miles out into the ocean. Sea ice, too, reflects solar energy back toward space.

The deepest cold is measured in winter, when little sunlight falls on Antarctica. At the South Pole, the sun sinks below the horizon in mid-March and does not reappear until mid-September. For many weeks the huge continent is lit only by stars, the moon, and the shimmering *aurora australis*, or southern lights.

In 1983 the coldest temperature measured on earth—128 degrees below zero, Fahrenheit—was recorded on Antarctica. This is colder than the surface of Mars. At this temperature, water thrown into the air freezes before it hits the ground.

In the Antarctic interior, sub-zero temperatures and fierce winds test the stamina of scientists.

Antarctica is called a "heat sink" by scientists who study climate. Warm air masses from other continents are quickly chilled in the Antarctic. Although the forces that affect world climate are not completely understood, scientists agree that Antarctica has a major influence on the weather of the entire earth. It affects winds in the atmosphere and currents in the oceans.

When people see a snow- or ice-covered landscape, they assume that the land gets lots of precipitation. This is not true of either the Antarctic or Arctic. Both are deserts, with only a few inches of precipitation a year. Almost no snow falls in the interior of Antarctica. The coasts receive more, and as much as 30 inches of precipitation (both snow and rain) sometimes falls on the Antarctic Peninsula.

The peninsula has the warmest climate of the Antarctic continent. Its northern tip is just 600 miles from the southern tip of South America. Along the peninsula's northwest, summer temperatures sometimes reach 59 degrees Fahrenheit.

By Antarctic standards, this is very warm, so that part of the peninsula is sometimes called the "banana belt."

Antarctic snow usually falls as pellets, not flakes. Often what seems like a raging blizzard is just loose, already-fallen snow being blown about on the earth's windiest continent. Winds can reach 200 miles an hour. Inland research stations are quickly buried by wind-driven snow. And snow drifts sometimes conceal potential deathtraps: crevasses, hundreds of feet deep, that scar the surface of Antarctica's ice sheets.

Snowfalls of millions of years have changed to ice that is now two to three miles deep in the center of two ice sheets. The ice sheets are divided by the Transantarctic Mountains. Except for the tallest mountains and some land along the coasts, all of the Antarctic continent is hidden by ice, and pressed down by its weight. Most of the land has been pushed below sea level; it is Antarctica's ice that makes it the earth's highest continent.

The ice moves. Slowly but steadily, it slips downward and outward from the center of the continent. Buildings on the surface move toward

The Transantarctic Mountains

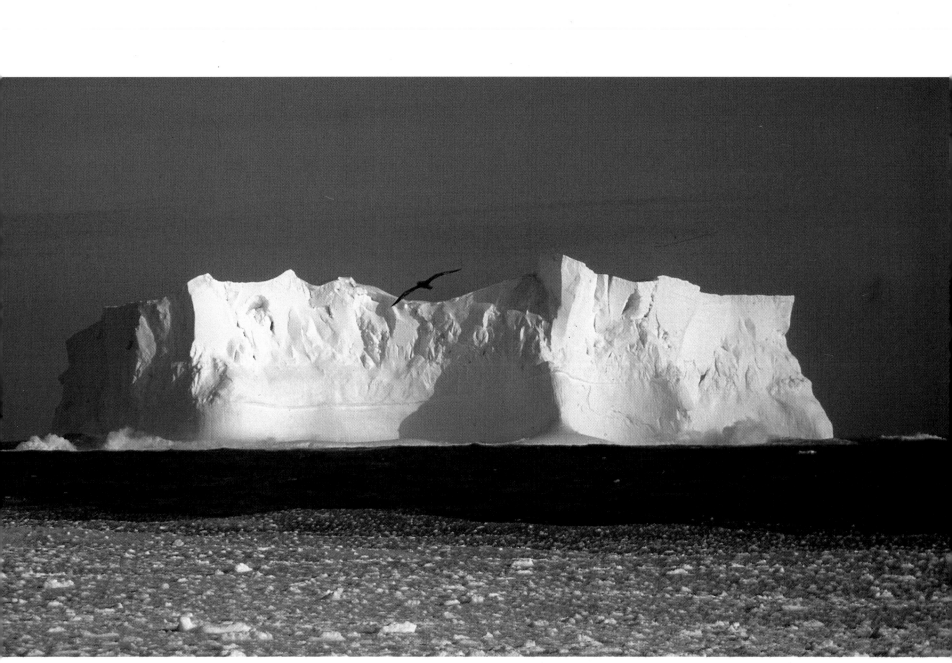

Icebergs drift for years in Antarctic waters.

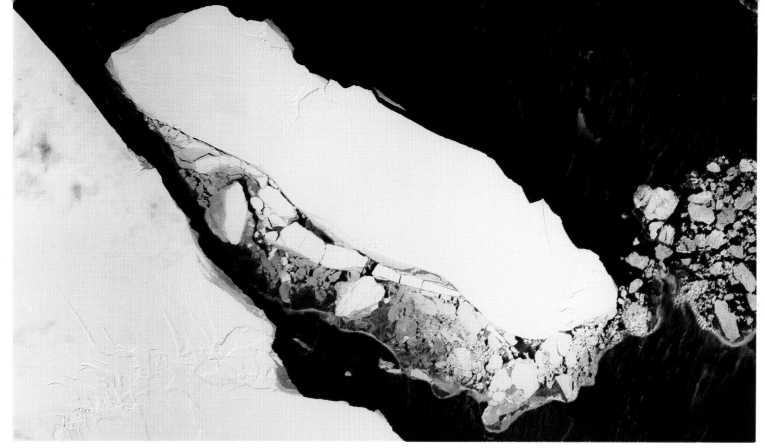

Icebergs can be as big as a house, a city, or in the case of B-9, shown in this satellite photo, as big as a small state.

the sea at a pace of about 33 feet a year. At the coast, chunks break off and float away. Icebergs also break, or "calve," from seven major glaciers. Most icebergs (all of the largest ones) calve from ice shelves, which move seaward at the rate of a half mile a year.

At first these icebergs are shaped like tables, with flat tops. They melt into irregular, unusual shapes. The largest iceberg known was found in 1956 near the Ross Ice Shelf. It was 201 miles long and 58 miles wide—nearly the size of Massachusetts and Connecticut combined.

In 1987 another huge iceberg broke from the Ross Ice Shelf. B-9, as it was called, was about the size of the state of Delaware. Until it began to break up, in 1989, it was 96 miles long, 22 miles wide, and 750 feet deep. B-9 contained an estimated 287 cubic miles of fresh water. That is enough to give everyone on earth two glasses of water a day for 1,977 years.

Fossils found in rocks of insects (above), dinosaurs, and trees reveal that Antarctica's climate was much warmer in the past.

CLUES TO THE PAST, AND TO THE FUTURE

Early in this century, Swedish geologists found fossil wood and leaf imprints of fig, beech, and sequoia trees in Antarctica. This was evidence that the continent had once been forested, with a much warmer climate.

Many other fossils of Antarctica's past life have been discovered. They include stumps of evergreen trees, shark teeth, bones of a small mammal, and also those of turtles, fish, whales, and dolphins. In 1989 and 1990, dinosaur bones were found on the Antarctic Peninsula and on a mountain just 400 miles from the South Pole. These fossils help scientists picture the climate and landscape of the Antarctic millions of years ago.

Two discoveries were especially significant. One was the skeleton of a 5-foot-long reptile, called Lystrosaurus. The second, found in 1986, was the beak of a tall, flightless "terror bird." It was discovered on an island near the Antarctic Peninsula.

These two fossils link Antarctica to other continents. Lystrosaurus bones have been unearthed in South Africa and India. Terror bird fossils have been dug up in South America and Florida.

Neither of these animals was a long distance swimmer, so the location of their fossil remains on several continents is evidence that the continents were once all connected. In fact, some geologists believe that Antarctica once lay alongside North America, when all land masses were joined in one supercontinent.

It began to break up about 190 million years ago. In a process called continental drift, different land masses began to move apart, carried on gigantic plates that form the earth's crust. Australia and Antarctica separated about 55 million years ago. Antarctica moved toward the South Pole, and there became surrounded by cold ocean currents. Antarctica's forests died out and ice sheets began to form.

Like fossils in rocks, the ice itself holds clues to

the past. As a snowflake forms and falls to earth it becomes a small sample of the chemistry of the atmosphere. Antarctic ice sheets represent a record of many, many past snowfalls. A core of ice drilled by Soviet scientists goes back 180,000 years. (The drill uses an electrically heated ring to melt its way down, leaving a central cylinder of ice that can be lifted to the surface.) This and other ice cores, collected in Antarctica and Greenland, contain information about the earth's climate and environment, long ago and more recently.

Within ice cores lie traces of past volcanic erup-

tions, and lightweight pollen grains carried by winds from other continents. The flowering plants that produced the pollen can be identified, and the types of plants are clues to past climates.

When chemists analyze air trapped in tiny bubbles within ice cores, they find a reliable record of changes in the amounts of certain gases. They are learning, for example, how the amount of carbon dioxide in the atmosphere has changed. Molecules of this gas absorb heat and warm the earth's atmosphere. Studies of ice cores show that carbon dioxide levels are increasing. (So are levels of methane, another gas that traps heat in the earth's atmosphere.)

Special drills reach deep into Antarctica's ice and remove ice cores that contain ancient samples of the earth's air. Inside an unheated plastic tent (left), scientists are protected from the wind while ice cores are kept cold.

By burning coal and other fuels, people add more and more carbon dioxide to the earth's atmosphere. This causes global warming—perhaps one of the most challenging problems facing humans today. To help solve this problem, people need a better understanding of our planet's climate, both now and in the past. Fortunately, the best information about earth's climate is recorded in the ice sheets of Antarctica.

The West Antarctic ice sheet is being watched to see whether it will be affected by global warming. Parts of it rest on the sea floor, and are less stable than the ice on land. Rising ocean temperatures might cause large parts of the ice sheet to float free. This would cause sea levels to rise sharply all over the world, flooding low-lying coastal areas.

For some scientific studies, central Antarctica is the best research site on earth. Nearly ten thousand meteorite fragments have been found there, mostly in places where winds wear away ice and expose them to view. Scientists are studying this unusual trove of meteorites. One came from the moon, and two others may be from Mars.

The plateau around the South Pole is now recog-

Balloons that rise more than 20 miles above Antarctica carry instruments that detect gamma rays from the sun.

nized as ideal for astronomy. It is the highest and driest desert in the world, with almost no water vapor to interfere with observation of the sun and stars. Three large telescopes will soon be built there, as Antarctica becomes a vital center for study of cosmic rays, the formation of stars, the earth's magnetic fields, and the origin of the universe.

Meteorites fall everywhere on earth but are especially easy to spot on Antarctica's ice. Below, a view from space of the southern lights, aurora australis, over Antarctica.

Surrounded by vast ice sheets, Antarctica's dry valleys still harbor simple forms of life. Above, a band of lichens grows just beneath the surface of a sandstone rock.

LIFE ON LAND

From its desolate interior to its surrounding seas, Antarctica is a natural laboratory that offers unique opportunities for research on plants and animals. When space explorers from Earth set foot on Mars, they probably will have trained on Antarctica. They certainly will benefit from studies of its Mars-like climate. For example, they will know where to look for signs of present or past plant life on Mars.

In the rock-strewn and ice-free dry valleys of central Antarctica, it is easy to assume that no plants survive the bitter cold. However, if you picked up a piece of sandstone rock and split it apart with a hammer, you might see a narrow band of green just below the surface. This green band is made up of lichens, plants that are part fungus, part algae. Lichens are hardy plants, but they cannot survive out in the open on surfaces that may freeze and thaw several times during an Antarctic summer day.

Just beneath the rock surface, the climate (a microclimate) is warmer, more stable, and more humid. Lichens thrive in the tiny air spaces of porous sandstone. They get nutrients from the rocks. Light, air, and traces of water from melted snow reach the microscopic spaces within the rocks. In addition to lichens, scientists have found bacteria, yeasts, and blue-green algae living inside rocks.

Even the snow and ice of Antarctica sometimes harbor plant life. In northern coastal areas during the summer, snow is often stained red, green, or yellow by algae.

Antarctica coastal regions are home for many species of lichen, moss, and liverworts. Although lichens survive within 300 miles of the South Pole, the most abundant plant life on the continent occurs along the coasts and especially on the Antarctic Peninsula. Lush beds of mosses grow on the peninsula, which is home to Antarctica's only

In summertime, algae colors the snow near the coast.

two species of flowering plants–hair grass and pearlwort.

After a visit to the South Pole, author Barry Lopez wrote, "The wind is the only animal that lives here." The animal life of the continent is as sparse as that of plants. The largest animal that lives year round on land is a midge that measures a half inch long. (Usually, midges can fly, but wings can be troublesome for an insect on earth's windiest continent; this species is wingless.)

Other Antarctic land animals include spider-like mites and insects called springtails.

Two-thirds of all insects on the continent are parasites, living on the bodies of Antarctica's warm-blooded birds and mammals, whose home is mostly sea and ice, not land. The parasites include biting lice on birds, sucking lice on seals, and fleas on petrels.

Microscopic plants and animals live in some Antarctic lakes, but probably not in the continent's biggest lakes. These bodies of water lie under more than 10,000 feet of ice, and were only detected with echo-sounding devices.

On the continent's surface, some small lakes are located in the dry valleys. One called Don Juan Pond is thirteen times more salty than sea water, and never freezes. Most Antarctic lakes are usually frozen to a depth of ten feet, even in summer. Nevertheless, some sunlight penetrates the ice to a zone of freshwater, where microscopic animals and plants live.

Antarctic is treeless. Its most lush plant life— including mosses, lichens, and just one kind of grass— grows on the Antarctic Peninsula.

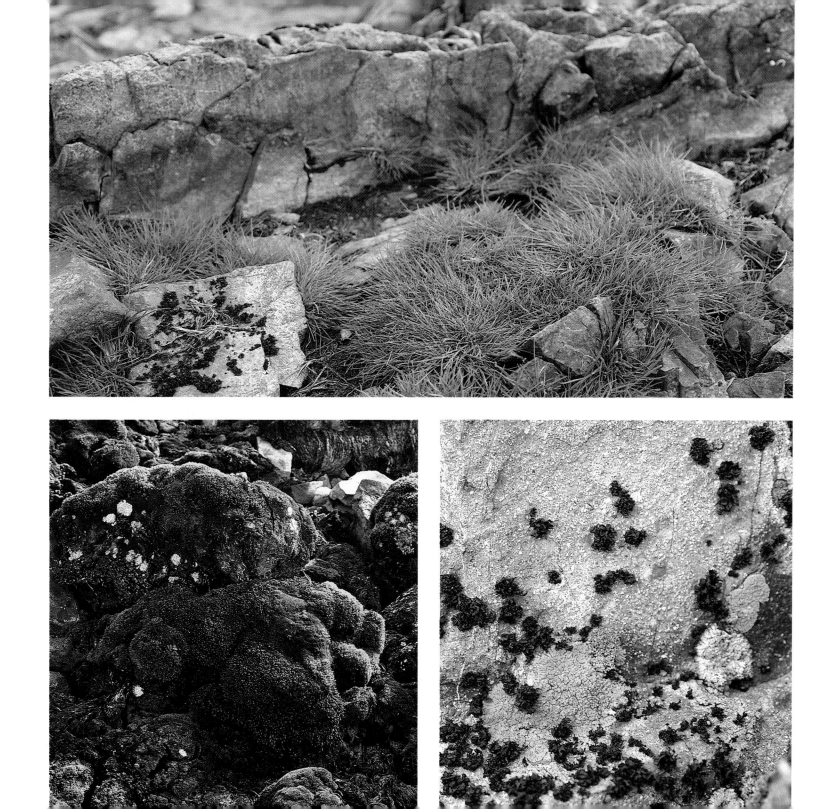

Adelie penguins gather for a few weeks each year to raise young in nests made of rings of pebbles. Parents regurgitate food (above) for their young.

AT THE OCEAN'S EDGE

*I*t is at the edges of the Antarctic continent, where land or ice meet the sea, that wildlife is concentrated. Penguins and seals find their food in the water, but killer whales or leopard seals may also lurk there.

Penguins need the safety of land or ice on which to rest and raise their young. On land penguins have no natural enemies. They don't fear people. Most people find penguins the most appealing birds on earth. They are surprised to learn that, in the nineteenth century, penguins were slaughtered by the millions for meat and for lamp oil from their boiled bodies. The populations of Antarctic penguins have since recovered. They now total at least a hundred million.

Seven penguin species live on the shores of the continent and on nearby islands: Adelie, gentoo, macaroni, chinstrap, rockhopper, king, and emperor. The Adelie (named after the wife of a

French explorer) is the smallest, most abundant, and most widely distributed. The emperor is the biggest, standing about three and a half feet tall. (Fossil bones of an extinct larger penguin, nearly five feet tall, have been found on Antarctica.)

The breeding cycles of most penguins, and other seabirds, are closely tied to the natural food supply. Egg-laying is usually timed so that the hatching and rapid growth of young birds coincides with high populations of crustaceans and other foods. Some gull-like skuas make their nests near penguin colonies, and raise their young while the penguins are also nesting. Skuas eat penguin eggs and young, so the colony is a handy food supply for their own chicks.

Some seabirds, including the wandering albatross and king and emperor penguins, lay their eggs after all of the other birds have finished rearing their young. Their chicks are raised in the dark, frigid winter.

Colonies of emperor penguins gather to breed on sea ice, in the shelter of ice cliffs. Females lay a single egg, then waddle off to the sea. Each male penguin balances an egg on his feet and keeps it warm with a special fold of skin. There is nothing to eat. For more than two months the birds survive on stored fat.

In the worst weather, emperor penguins form

Hunting for food for their own young, some skuas prey on Adelie penguin chicks and eggs.

Emperor penguins stand nearly four feet tall.

huddles of as many as 5,000 birds. A huddle of penguins moves slowly. Individual birds shift position, sometimes exposed to the wind, sometimes snug in the center. In this way, no bird is continually exposed to the icy breath of winter winds.

About the time the eggs hatch, the mother birds return. They regurgitate food for the chicks and keep them warm while the males trek over the ice to the nearest open water. It may be more than a hundred miles away, and many days pass before the males return with food. In some winters, many chicks starve to death. In others, the sea ice begins to break up early and the parent birds don't have to travel far to catch plenty of food for their young.

Awkward and slow on land, penguins move swiftly and gracefully underwater. King penguins have dived as deep as 825 feet. Some penguins catch small fish, but all Antarctic species feed mostly on krill. These shrimp-like crustaceans are also eaten by petrels, terns, albatrosses, and other seabirds. Many seabirds hunt at night, when krill and other prey rise close to the surface.

Krill are also a vital food for some of the seals that live in Antarctica. The crabeater seal, despite its name, feeds mostly on krill. Its remarkable cheek teeth act like strainers. The seal grabs a mouthful of water filled with krill, then expels the water and keeps the krill to swallow.

The leopard seal depends on krill and other small prey for about half of its food. Its teeth also strain tiny crustaceans from the water, but the leopard seal's bigger, sharper teeth also enable it to kill young crabeater seals. Its large jaws gape wide and gobble down small penguins.

Leopard, crabeater, and Ross seals live on sea ice, sometimes far from the continent. Weddell seals live close to the Antarctic coast year round.

Crabeater seals at rest on sea ice.

All through the dark of winter they are under the ice. Weddell seals dive 2,000 feet in search of fish and squid. Being mammals, they must breathe air, so they gnaw away ice to keep breathing holes open.

Populations of elephant seals and fur seals are centered around islands north of Antarctica. These seals have recovered after being nearly wiped out by hunters a century ago. Fur seals may, in fact, be even more numerous now than they were when Captain James Cook saw hordes of their ancestors on island shores in the 1770s.

A mother Weddell seal and its young at a breathing hole she gnaws in the ice.

A Weddell seal

A leopard seal kills an Adelie penguin.

The rich life of Antarctica's surrounding seas depends on isopods and other small crustaceans.

LIFE OF THE SURROUNDING SEAS

In Antarctica, scientists study habitats found nowhere else on earth. One unusual environment lies beneath the Ross Ice Shelf, which floats on sea water up to a thousand feet deep. What might live in the water beneath the ice, in a world of constant darkness?

In one study, a hole was drilled through 1,390 feet of ice to reach water under the ice shelf. Television cameras and baited traps were lowered to see or catch the animals, if any, that live there. The scientists saw and captured small crustaceans called amphipods and isopods. They also photographed a fish that appeared to be one of the same kinds that live in the Ross Sea. Somehow, these creatures eke out a living in darkness, 258 miles from the open sea.

Scientists who have dived and explored the Antarctic sea floor close to shore find that it is too scraped and battered by ice for many plants or animals to survive. But farther offshore in the Southern Ocean they have discovered a bounty of living things.

The average temperature of the seawater is 28 degrees Fahrenheit. This is the earth's coldest ocean, but it is rich in oxygen. It is also rich in nutrients carried by currents that well up from deep in the Southern Ocean.

The rocky sea floor itself is a garden of seaweeds, corals, sponges, and anemones. Starfish, limpets, sea slugs, and sea urchins cling or crawl about. Sea spiders feed on the anemones.

Adapted to cold year-round temperatures, Antarctic fishes are slow-growing and long-lived. They have chemicals in their blood and body fluids that keep ice crystals from forming. (Scientists are still trying to learn how these anti-freeze chemicals work and whether these substances might be useful in human medicine.)

The most unusual Antarctic fish lacks hemoglobin, which is a red-colored substance in blood that carries oxygen. All other animals with backbones, including people, have hemoglobin in their blood. The Antarctic fish lacking it have white gills, and are called ice fish. To supply their cells with oxygen they have more blood, larger blood vessels, and larger, faster-beating hearts than other fish. These characteristics enable ice fish to use less energy when resting than fish with hemoglobin.

Ice on the ocean surface affects the life cycles of many sea organisms. Snow on ice reflects most sunlight, and shuts off the supply of solar energy to the water below. When no snow covers the ice, sunlight can pass through. It gives energy to algae populations that bloom just beneath the ice. The algae are eaten by krill and other small organisms.

The continuous daylight of summer melts away much ice, and fuels an explosion of life in the Southern Ocean. Microscopic plants called diatoms flourish. About a hundred species of diatoms make up most of the phytoplankton—drifting microscopic plants. The diatoms are eaten by zooplankton—tiny aquatic animals. In Antarctic waters the most abundant zooplankton are tiny crustaceans called copepods and the larger krill. Of eleven krill species, the biggest one—1½ inches long—is most common.

In summer, krill feed near the surface in huge swarms that tint the ocean water red. Krill are a key link in many Antarctic food chains. The krill themselves eat other zooplankton, bacteria, and phytoplankton. They, in turn, are eaten by penguins, other seabirds, seals, and whales. Krill are also a key part of longer food chains, being eaten by fishes and squid, which are later eaten by

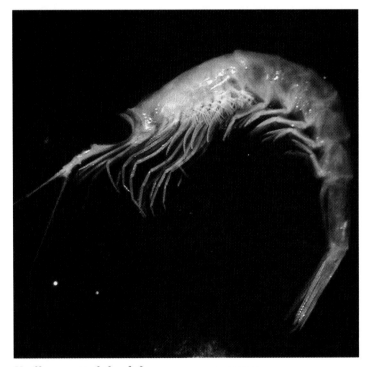

Krill are vital food for many creatures, from small fish to mighty whales.

The sea floor near Antarctica teems with life, including anemones (above), ice fish, and brittle star fish.

The lives of right whales and other baleen whales depend on summer feasting in Antarctic waters.

Baleen bristles strain plankton from the water.

larger animals. Ross seals and king penguins, for example, eat many squid. So their lives depend indirectly on krill.

As the Antarctic summer begins, whales leave warmer waters and swim thousands of miles to feast on krill and other zooplankton. The whales—blue, fin, sei, minke, right, and humpback—are called baleen whales. They have hard plates on the sides of their mouths, called baleen. The plates are fringed with fine bristles that act as food strainers. Baleen strains krill and other zooplankton from water that the whales engulf.

The right whale sometimes swims with its head

partway out of the water and its mouth half-open. When it has trapped enough krill it closes its mouth and swallows them. Humpback whales have been observed "herding" krill. A whale circles a krill swarm, causing them to swim into a more compact group. Then the whale dives and rises up beneath the concentrated krill with its mouth open.

For eights months of the year, baleen whales live far from the Southern Ocean. Their survival, however, depends on the food energy they store while in Antarctic waters. Toothed whales also depend on the bounty of food in these waters. Sperm whales and southern bottlenose whales dive deep and hunt for squid. Killer whales also catch squid, as well as fish, seals, and Adelie penguins.

The lives of all these creatures, from 2-foot-tall penguins to 100-foot-long whales, depend on plankton, and the nutrients and deep, cold, clear waters that surround Antarctica.

Killer whales

Open air burning of wastes has been stopped at the U.S. McMurdo Station but continues at other nations' bases.

THE HUMAN IMPACT

With its oddly sculpted icebergs, its bone-chilling cold, and the braying, hissing, and trumpeting sounds of its penguins, Antarctica seems like another planet. But there is plenty of evidence that it is part of this world: trash heaps, an oil spill, and global air pollution that may threaten the bountiful life of the Southern Ocean.

Beginning with the first explorers, people have brought all sorts of stuff to Antarctica and left it there. The huts of early expeditions still remain. Remarkably, so do the partly-decayed bodies of sled dogs that died nearly a century ago. Dead animals, sewage, and other organic material decay very slowly in Antarctica's cold, dry climate.

Visitors enjoying the pristine beauty of Antarctica are often jolted when they reach one of several dozen bases and research stations along the rocky coast. Some look like ugly mining towns, surrounded with discarded machinery and other trash. For many years, masses of solid waste were dragged out onto the sea ice, and sank when summer came. Divers have found the seafloor covered with rubbish, from tractors to beer cans, more than three miles from McMurdo Station, the main United States base.

The United States contaminated part of its McMurdo base with nuclear wastes. A small nuclear reactor generated heat and electricity for nearly eleven years. It was shut down in 1972, taken apart, and shipped back to the United States. But a problem remained: radiation had leaked into more than 12,000 tons of gravel and soil. This too was removed from Antarctica, at a cost of several million dollars.

The 1970s brought a new awareness all over the world of human impact on nature. Some of the Antarctic Treaty nations have since taken steps to protect the environment near their bases. In 1987 the United States began shipping some scrap metal, used oil, and other waste from Antarctica.

Environmental groups pressed the National Science Foundation, which administers U.S. Antarctic research, to do more. Trash that had been discarded at the McMurdo site (first occupied in 1901) is gradually being removed. A sewage treatment plant was built. McMurdo Station's staff and researchers—1,300 people in the summer—now sort their trash, separating recyclable materials that are shipped to the United States.

Batteries, and barrels filled with wastes, ready for shipment from Antarctica.

At McMurdo Station and other bases there have been fuel spills, but the worst accident of this kind occurred in 1989. An Argentine supply ship ran aground near the U.S. Palmer Station, on the Antarctic Peninsula, spilling more than 170,000 gallons of jet and diesel fuel. The fuel killed krill and wildlife, and also ruined some long term animal population studies.

On Antarctica, sheltered ice-free places on the rocky coast are prized by both humans and wildlife. Several research stations have disrupted penguin colonies. In 1983, the French began blasting away rocks to build an airstrip for its research base. The construction threatened nesting areas of petrels, Adelie penguins, and other birds. After protests by scientists and environmental groups, the project was postponed, but not cancelled.

Nesting seabirds can be disturbed by people visiting their colonies. An Adelie penguin population on Ross Island, near McMurdo Station, declined sharply after 1956. Helicopters carrying scientists, journalists, politicians, and other visitors landed near the penguins. People were allowed to roam among the nesting penguins.

The birds' normal routine was upset, and their numbers dropped by half in a few years. Fortunately, the problem was recognized in time. The helicopter landing site was changed, and visitors

were kept a respectful distance from the nesting birds. Penguin numbers then began to rise.

Antarctica is a rugged, wild place, but it is also a fragile place. Nature in a cold desert world like this is slow to recover. For example, plants grow very slowly, so bootprints in a bed of moss stay visible for several years. The effects of other, more serious human impacts, like oil spills, are also likely to be long-lasting.

Some scientists and environmentalists worry about the effects of Antarctic tourists. Each year, about 3,000 tourists visit parts of the Antarctic coast by ship. Most of them care about nature, and about protecting the Antarctic environment. Nevertheless, their visits can do harm. Their landings on shore are concentrated in a few areas, mostly on the Antarctic Peninsula. Summer is Antarctica's only season for tourism; it is also the only season for seals, seabirds, and most penguins to raise their young. The tourism industry may have to be regulated in order to protect Antarctica's plants and animals, and its wildness.

Scientists are also concerned about threats to Antarctica's value as a unique vantage point for

Penguins and people compete for sheltered sites along the rocky coast.

Tourists visit an abandoned whaling station, where whales were once slaughtered, on an island near Antarctica.

studies of the earth's atmosphere and climate. That value depends on Antarctica's wild isolation and its air quality—the least polluted on earth. The pristine air is already threatened. At McMurdo Station, for example, trash in the dump was burned. The refuse was doused with thousands of gallons of waste fuel, adding further pollutants to the air. Environmental groups and atmospheric scientists urged that this practice be stopped. It was, in 1990; but open dump burning will not stop at all research stations until 1999.

In late 1991, technicians at McMurdo used 400 pounds of explosives to blow up a stockpile of dis-

carded chemicals. The National Science Foundation claimed that the chemicals had been too unstable to be shipped safely from Antarctica. In the United States, this blast would have been illegal because there had been no study of its possible effects on the air, or wildlife. Environmental groups criticized the National Science Foundation for scattering toxic chemicals into the Antarctic winds.

In the early 1980s, British scientists detected a "hole" in the layer of ozone that surrounds the earth, high in the stratosphere. This thinning of the ozone layer has since been confirmed by observations from satellites and aircraft. Ozone shields the earth from most harmful incoming ultraviolet rays. Ultraviolet radiation from the sun can cause skin cancer and other health problems in humans, and also harm plants and animals.

The loss of protective ozone is caused by chemicals called chlorofluorocarbons, or CFCs. They were widely used in industrial nations as coolant gases in air conditioners and refrigerators, and as propellant gases in spray cans. The use of CFCs is being phased out, but these long-lasting gases continue to drift up to the stratosphere. There, chlorine atoms from CFCs destroy more ozone.

The ozone layer has been depleted all over the earth, but the extreme winter cold in the atmosphere over the South Pole seems to allow chlorine atoms to cause the greatest thinning there. It may be an early warning of conditions that might develop in other places. The ozone hole appears over Antarctica in August and reaches its greatest extent in October (spring in the Southern Hemisphere). It has grown deeper, and concern about its effects has also deepened. Some research shows that increased ultraviolet light slows the food-making of diatoms and other phytoplankton. Some kinds of microscopic plants die when they are exposed to an increase in ultraviolet radiation. Other kinds are not so sensitive.

Scientists have many questions about the ozone hole and its effects on life. Once again, Antarctica is the outdoor laboratory where these questions can be answered. In this case, however, increasing ultraviolet light is much more than a scientific curiosity. It might be a threat to the Antarctic's tiny water plants, and to the krill and all of the other animals that depend on them for life.

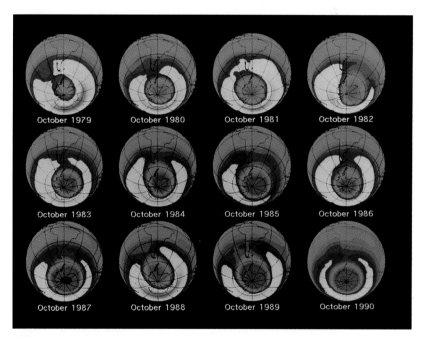

The ozone layer over Antarctica, thinnest in October, grew thinner during the 1980s and early 1990s. Orange-yellow indicates high amounts of ozone; dark purple, low amounts.

*A geologist studies
the rocks of an
Antarctic mountain range,
where deposits
of coal have been found.*

A TURNING POINT

The Antarctic Treaty did not expire in 1991. Under article XII of the treaty, however, an opportunity for review and change was provided after June 1991. Any of the original twelve nations that signed the treaty, or others that had established research stations on Antarctica, could call for a meeting of all. And any proposed change would require unanimous approval of all of these nations.

Interest in possessing land in Antarctica is still very much alive. A group of 77 nations that have no research bases on Antarctica have declared that they, too, have to be considered when the continent's resources are developed.

Argentina went to unusual lengths to strengthen its territorial claims. A pregnant woman was flown to one of its bases. She gave birth to a baby boy in January 1978—the first human birth on Antarctica. Then Argentine soldiers at Antarctic bases were allowed to have their wives with them. More Argentine "natives" of Antarctica have since been born. The government grants them Argentine citizenship.

The treaty had succeeded because it shelved territorial claims, and also because it ignored the issues of fishing rights in the Southern Ocean and mining rights on the continent. Overfishing by the former Soviet Union has already depleted stocks of Antarctic cod, ice fish, and other species. The Soviets and Japanese have also netted up to a half-million tons of krill a year. Most krill is used as food for livestock, but foods for people made from krill have also been developed.

In 1988, after six years of negotiations, thirty-three nations worked out a set of rules concerning the mineral resources of Antarctica. Prospecting for minerals and oil would be allowed, but large-scale exploration or development would have to be

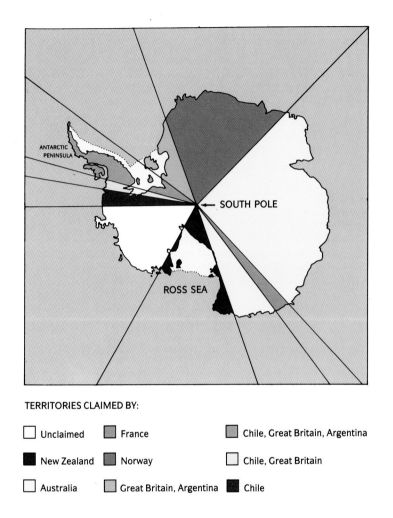

ANTARCTIC
PENINSULA

SOUTH POLE

ROSS SEA

TERRITORIES CLAIMED BY:

☐ Unclaimed	▨ France	▨ Chile, Great Britain, Argentina
■ New Zealand	▨ Norway	☐ Chile, Great Britain
☐ Australia	▨ Great Britain, Argentina	■ Chile

approved by all treaty nations with voting rights. However, two of the Antarctic Treaty countries—France and Australia—refused to sign the accord. In 1989 they proposed that Antarctica be declared a wilderness reserve, to be watched over by an international environmental agency.

The idea of an Antarctic World Park was hailed by Greenpeace, the Natural Resources Defense Council, and nearly 200 other environmental groups in 35 countries. (In 1987, Greenpeace set up a permanent Antarctic base of its own. It is the first non-government organization to do so.) However, some nations opposed a permanent ban on oil and mineral development.

Negotiations continued, and in 1991 led to a new agreement that bans oil and mineral exploration in Antarctica for 50 years. This accord also included new rules for disposal of wastes (including those from ships), protection of plants and animals, and studies of the environmental impact of all projects in Antarctica.

Governments and environmentalists hailed this new protection for the earth's last great wilderness. Antarctica, however, is not yet a World Park. Overfishing threatens its stocks of fish and krill; crowds of tourists may harm its wildlife. And new rules on paper must lead to actions on Antarctica itself.

The treasure of Antarctica is of extraordinary value to everyone on earth. It is worth extraordinary cooperation by all nations to ensure that it remains unspoiled.

GLOSSARY

aurora   A shimmering display of many-colored lights in the night sky that is especially vivid in polar regions. It is a kind of electrical storm, caused by charged particles from the sun entering the earth's magnetic field. The aurora of the north is called aurora borealis, while that of the south is called aurora australis.

chlorofluorocarbons (CFCs)   Gases used as coolants in refrigerators and air conditioners, and as foaming agents for insulation and food packaging. In the upper atmosphere, chlorine from CFCs destroys ozone that protects life on earth from the sun's harmful ultraviolet radiation. Use of CFCs as propellant gases in aerosol cans has been halted in most nations, and there are international agreements to further reduce CFC production.

climate   The average long-term atmospheric conditions, including temperature, wind, and precipitation, that prevail in a particular place. Climates of small areas—like the north side of a tree trunk—are called microclimates.

continental drift   The process by which the earth's continents change position. About 200 million years ago they were joined in a single land mass. They continue to move and will change their positions. The continents and ocean basins are carried on 20 plates, about 60 miles thick, that make up the earth's crust.

fossils   Skeletons, tracks, or other traces of animals or plants from past ages that have been preserved in rock.

glacier   A huge mass of ice, formed from compacted snow, whose sides are often bounded by mountains or the walls of a valley. Ice sheets or caps, also formed from compacted snow, are so massive that they cover entire landscapes, mountains as well as valleys. Glaciers and ice sheets flow slowly toward the sea, where chunks break off and are called icebergs.

global warming   The gradual warming of the earth's atmosphere that most atmospheric scientists now believe is under way. Human activities that add carbon dioxide, methane, and other heat-trapping gases to the atmosphere may cause enough warming to raise sea levels, change rainfall patterns, and threaten crops, water supplies, wildlife, and coastal cities.

hemoglobin   An iron-containing pigment in blood that gives it a red color, and which carries oxygen to all cells of the body.

ice   Water frozen solid, ice occurs in its greatest variety in the coldest place on earth, the Antarctic. At least 78 different forms of ice have been named. They include bullet ice, frazil ice, grease ice, green ice, ice flowers, ice saddles, and pancake ice.

lichen   A "team" of two plants, an alga and a fungus, living together. The alga makes food, the fungus protects the alga from drying out. Lichens lack roots, stems, or leaves. They grow on rocks and tree bark.

meteorite Fragments of stone or iron (or both) that travel through space, circling the sun, are called meteoroids. Those that do not burn up in a planet's atmosphere and reach its surface are called meteorites.

ozone A form of oxygen present in the earth's atmosphere in small amounts. A layer of ozone, between fourteen and nineteen miles above sea level, makes life possible by shielding the earth's surface from most ultraviolet rays.

parasite An organism that lives on or in another organism, its host, sometimes harming it but usually not killing it. Parasites include fleas, ticks, lice, and tapeworms.

plankton Tiny drifting plants and animals of ponds, lakes, and oceans. Many are visible only through a microscope. Phytoplankton are plants that are the foundation of many food chains. Zooplankton are animals that feed mostly on phytoplankton, and are food themselves for larger animals.

ultraviolet radiation Invisible radiation from the sun that has shorter wavelengths than visible violet light. Ultraviolet light includes tanning rays, but also more powerful wavelengths that cause sunburn and skin cancer. Most of these harmful rays do not reach the earth's surface because they are blocked by a layer of ozone gas in the stratosphere.

PICTURE CREDITS

Maps by Sylvia Frezzolini Severance. Photos: Doug Allan, Oxford Scientific Films, p. 41 (right); Canterbury Museum, p. 11; Earth Observation Satellite Company, p. 21; Stan Jacobs, pp. 6, 7, 9, 24, 44; Dietland Muller-Schwarz, endpapers, title page, 4, 8, 13, 14 (top), 32, 33, 34, 35, 53; National Aeronautics & Space Administration, pp. 16, 27 (bottom), 49; National Science Foundation, pp. 19, 22, 25, 26, 27 (top), 28, 41 (left), 43, 46, 50; Russell Petro, pp. 31 (top & lower right), 48; Susan Petro, pp. 30, 37 (left), 47. Photos from Visuals Unlimited: Frank Awbrey, p. 31 (lower left); Jim Harvey, p. 42 (bottom); G. Prance, p. 36; Kjell Sandved, p. 37 (lower right), 38; Marty Snyderman, p. 42 (top); Jeanette Thomas, pp. 2-3, 14 (bottom), 15, 18, 20, 37 (top right); Adrian Wenner, p. 40.

INDEX